DATE DUE

Demco, Inc. 38-293

RACE CAR LEGENDS

The Allisons

Mario Andretti

Crashes & Collisions

Drag Racing

Dale Earnhardt

Formula One Racing

A.J. Foyt

Jeff Gordon

Motorcycles

Richard Petty

The Unsers

Women in Racing

CHELSEA HOUSE PUBLISHERS

RACE CAR LEGENDS

WOMEN IN RACING

Michael Benson

CHELSEA HOUSE PUBLISHERS

Philadelphia

Produced by Daniel Bial and Associates
New York, New York

Picture research by Alan Gottlieb
Cover illustration and design by Robert Gerson
Cover photo credit: AP/Wide World Photos

Frontispiece photo: Patty Moise

First Printing

1 3 5 7 9 8 6 4 2

Library of Congress Cataloging-in-Publication Data

Benson, Michael.
    Women in racing / Michael Benson.
       p.   cm. -- (Race car legends)
    Includes bibiliographical references and index.
    Summary: A look at some of the women who have made their mark in
    the previously male-dominated sport of automobile racing, including
    Janet Guthrie, Lyn St. James, and Shawna Robinson.
    ISBN 0-7910-4432-7
       1. Women automobile racing drivers--Biography--Juvenile
literature.   [1. Automobile racing drivers.   2. Women--Biography.]
I.Title.   II. Series.
GV1032.A1B38   1997
796.72'092'2--dc21
[B]   97-14226
                                                                  CIP
                                                                  AC

CONTENTS

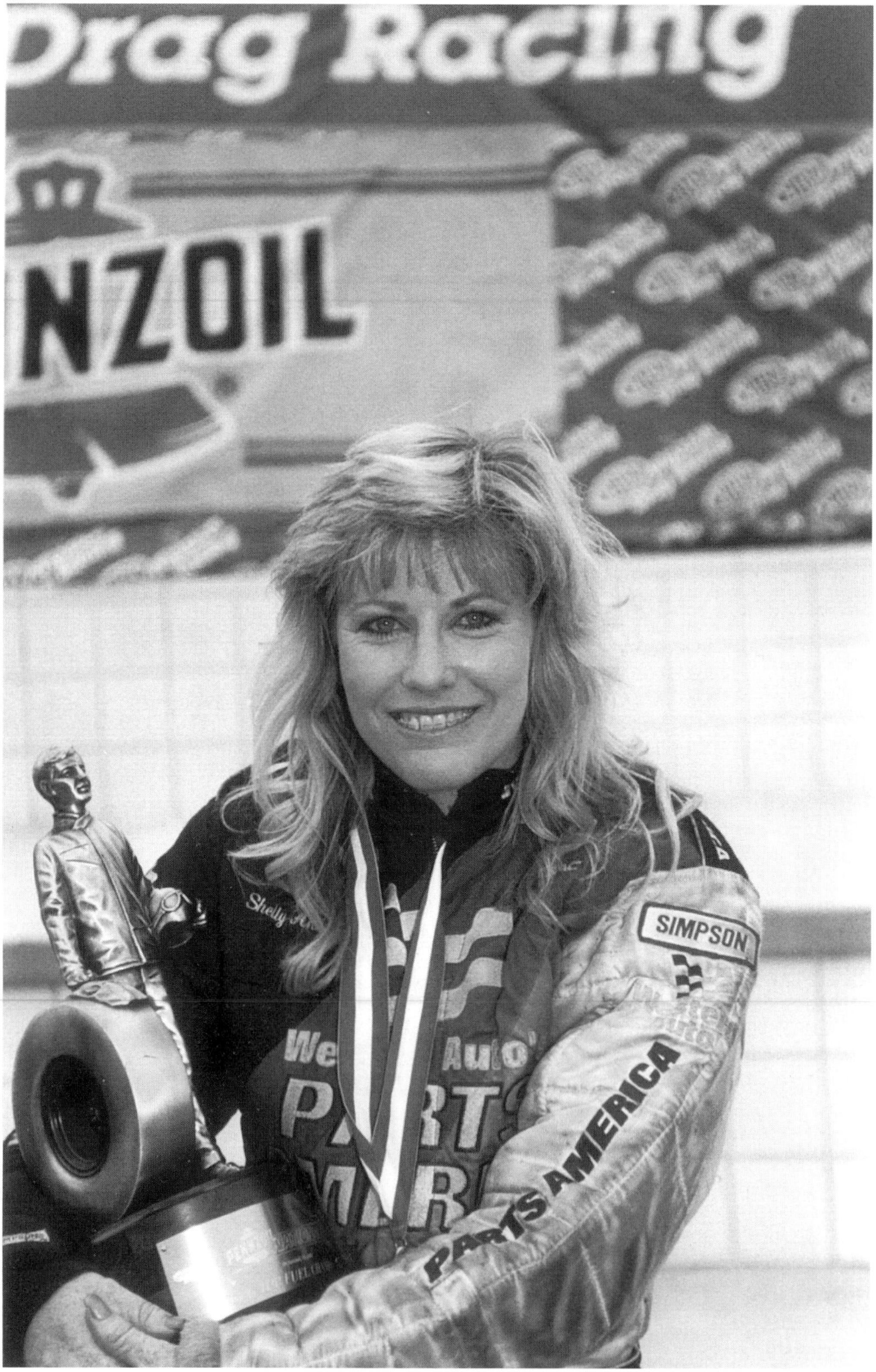
Drag Racing
NZOIL
SIMPSON
PARTS AMERICA

INTRODUCTION

Auto racing has long been a male-dominated sport. Look down the list of the big-time winners of NASCAR, Indy cars, and Formula 1 racing, and you will see names like Lee Petty, Terry Labonte, Lake Speed, Kelly Pitillo, Mauri Rose, Pat Flaherty, Arie Luyendyk, Niki Lauda, Kiki Rosberg, and Jackie Stewart—but these are all men.

Not only are the drivers mostly male, but also so are the members of the pit crew, the team owners, the race officials, and the track owners. But this is not to say that men are the only ones to race.

Women have been racing cars for nearly 100 years, since the beginning of automotive history. The first female race-car driver that we know of is a Mme. Labrouse of Paris, France, who drove in the Tour de France in 1899. Camille du Gast raced with 170 male drivers from Paris to Berlin in 1901 and she finished 33rd. Two years later, Camille raced from Paris to Madrid against 274 men and finished eighth. In Formula 1 (Grand Prix) racing, Lella Lombardi raced an entire season in 1975.

Today, women are involved at all levels of the racing world. Many of them have had to fight prejudiced male thinking that says a woman can never be as good as a man at such a masculine pursuit. But cars don't know who's driving them. And winning has nothing to do with testosterone. Victory belongs to those with the greatest talent, knowledge, and will to triumph.

Women have been racing cars—and winning—for nearly 100 years. Here Shelley Anderson shows one of the trophies she's earned in her brilliant career.

JANET GUTHRIE: WILL OF IRON

On a hot Indiana day in 1977, Tony Hulman, owner of the Indianapolis Motor Speedway, gave the famous call to start the world's number one racing event. Except this year he dramatically altered the command: "In company with the first lady ever to qualify at Indianapolis," Hulman said, "gentlemen, start your engines."

Moments later, Janet Guthrie, along with 32 male drivers, took the green flag and headed into Turn One at Indy at 180 mph to start the Indianapolis 500. She was the first woman to ever do so.

Guthrie made history that day, although her race didn't go very well. The problems were not her fault: her white and green car kept breaking down. She had only managed to get a few "hot" laps in when she was forced to make a pit stop. The right side fuel pressure valve was indicating that the engine was using too much fuel.

Janet Guthrie straps in before the start of the 1976 Firecracker 400.

Soon thereafter, she had to come in for mechanical repairs for a second time. This time a sensor valve needed to be changed.

This is when things got really uncomfortable. While her car was getting fuel, some of the alcohol-based fuel that these special cars use spilled into Janet's cockpit and seeped through her blue and white flameproof driving suit. Methanol fires can be quite dangerous, as the flames are nearly invisible. As the fuel burned her skin, Guthrie knew that getting out of the car, taking off the suit, and cleaning herself off would mean that her day on the world's most famous racetrack was finished.

She didn't want to do that.

So she took the pain and stayed in her seat. Every once in a while she asked a member of her pit crew to soak her down with cold water to help ease the burning. Eventually they gave her a big red plastic container with a spout so that she could rinse herself down.

"If they fix the car," she said. "I'll get back in the race and run like I was never out of it."

Then she handed the empty red water container to a pit-crew member. "Somebody had better fill that up," she said, without a note of urgency.

Janet would eventually make nine pit stops. The car was never right. Finally, Guthrie and her crew decided to call it a day. Now, Janet had one thing on her mind, getting to a shower. The trouble was, there was only one shower on Gasoline Alley, the road through the infield that serves as a second home to the crews during May at Indy.

She finally found the shower and, later, feeling much better, she became the first driver ever

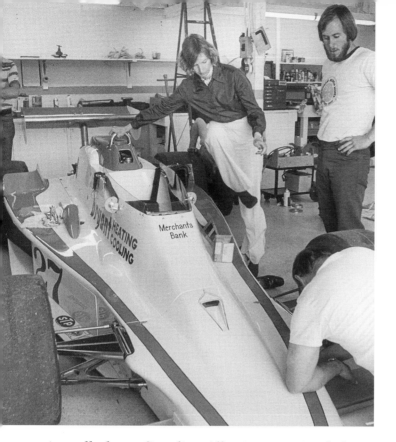

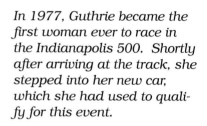

In 1977, Guthrie became the first woman ever to race in the Indianapolis 500. Shortly after arriving at the track, she stepped into her new car, which she had used to qualify for this event.

to walk down Gasoline Alley in open-toed shoes and painted toenails.

And the crowds cheered.

There were those, when the first woman qualified to race in the "Greatest Spectacle in Racing," who said that no female should ever drive at Indy. They thought that women didn't have the backbone, the guts, to compete in what had always before been a man's sport. But, by this simple gesture—staying in her seat even while blisters were forming on her skin from the spilled fuel—Janet Guthrie proved that women do have the guts to be race car drivers, even at the very highest level.

Guthrie was born in Iowa City, Iowa, but her family moved soon thereafter to Miami, Florida, where Janet grew up. Her parents told her that when she was just four, she was already on her bicycle heading for the horizon, making them chase her to bring her back. Janet can't remember if the story is true, but she does know that she has always been a thrill seeker.

After a year of arguing, she convinced her father—Lain Guthrie, a pilot for Eastern Airlines—to allow her to skydive when she was 16. She became an auto racer at 22. Her first race car was an XK120 Jaguar.

Becoming a race car driver was not her first choice, however. As a young woman, she dreamed of being an astronaut. She had the credentials. After graduating from the University of Michigan with a Bachelor of Science degree in physics, she worked for five years in the space program with Republic Aviation on Long Island when they were building space vehicles. She held a commercial pilot's license and had logged more than 400 hours of flight time in 23 different types of aircraft.

And, besides, the National Aeronautic Space Association (NASA) was looking to recruit a female astronaut. Janet applied and became one of four finalists, losing out eventually to Sally Ride.

Janet's first car races were gymkhanas, a competition in which cars, one at a time, weave their way through a pylon course against the clock. She excelled.

Before arriving in Indianapolis, Janet won several trophies and awards in French International (FIA) and Sports Car Club of America (SCCA) races, dating back to 1964. She raced in a dozen major endurance events, including the Watkins Glen 500 and the 24 Hours of Daytona. She won the Under Two-Litre Prototype class at the 12 Hours of Sebring in 1970 and competed a full season with the North Atlantic Road Racing circuit in 1973, winning their championship.

Before breaking the gender barrier at Indy, she had already competed in more than 120 road races, making her a good deal more experienced than the average Indy rookie.

Janet first drove an Indy car in 1976. That year she qualified 14th for the oval-track Indy-car race in Trenton in the Bryant Heating and Cooling Special for car-owner Rolla Vollstedt. She placed 15th in the race, dropping out early because of a broken gear box.

This performance was good enough to earn Janet the opportunity to take the rookie test for the Indianapolis 500. (The Indianapolis Motor Speedway is considered so dangerous that all rookies must pass a driving test before they are allowed to race there.) A. J. Foyt, a four-time champion at Indy, loaned her one of his backup cars, and she passed the rookie test by zooming around the track at a speed exceeding 181 mph.

Still, Janet would not get around to making a qualification attempt until the next year. Later in the 1976 season, she placed 24th in an Indy car race at Pocono, again dropping out with a gear box problem.

That season she qualified 12th for the Indy car race at Michigan, and, in the process, set a

At a press conference in 1978, Guthrie announced that Texaco was going to finance her car and crew at that year's running of the Indy 500.

women's closed-course speed record with a lap at 186.480 mph. She had been right among the leaders for much of the race until a flat tire ruined her chances and she finished 13th.

Then came 1977 and her first attempt to get into the field for the Indianapolis 500. During her first practice laps in the number 27 Lightning-Offenhauser car, again driving for car-owner Rolla Vollstedt, she was timed at an average speed of 191 mph. Then she hit the wall on May 10 and damaged the car. The car was repaired in time for her to successfully qualify at 188.404 mph, placing her in 16th place on the 33-car starting grid. The effort broke her own women's closed-course speed record.

After her successful qualifying run, she said, "I'd like to thank my folks for not bringing me up thinking that I couldn't do something because I'm a woman.

"Over the course of the year, I've given a lot of thought to the symbolism of being he first woman here [Indianapolis]. I think it is important to credit the women's movement with creating the climate that made this possible."

Hitting the wall at Indy at 190-plus is a terrifying experience, but if Janet felt fear she won't admit it.

"If you felt fear you would be a danger to yourself and to other drivers," she says. "You're concentrating—on what you're doing, what the other drivers are doing, what's happening on the track."

Why does she do it? Janet tries to explain:

"It's a challenge. Like the mountain-climbers' cliché: 'Because it's there.' I know of no other activity that calls upon you to extend yourself

100 percent on all levels—physical, emotional, intellectual, spiritual."

Janet never saw racing as a road to personal glory, although that was a pleasant side effect. She always enjoyed feeling that she was part of the fabric of a great team.

"The driver and the pit crew are only the tip of the iceberg," she explains. "You lose a machine part at 6:00 PM and you call the machinist, a member of the team whom the public never gets to see. Maybe he has worked all day, but he puts away his plans to take his wife to dinner and goes to the machine shop. He delivers the part to you at 6:00 AM the next morning."

Following Janet's gutsy but less than successful debut in the Indy 500, Lain Guthrie said of his daughter, "She's a smart girl. Don't know how she got involved in this. But she's always been strong. I remember when she was about three, I once told her, 'If you hurt yourself doing what I'm telling you not to do, I'll give you a spanking anyway.' She looked up and said, 'Doesn't sound right to me.' Will of iron."

Janet qualified for her second Indianapolis 500 in 1978 with an average speed of 190.325 mph. Her first lap again set the standard for women driving around a circuit; speed: 188.957. She started 15th and drove steadily for the entire race. She finished ninth, which remains to this day the best finish at Indy by a woman.

Janet did not race in any other Indy car races in 1978 and instead drove in the SCCA Trans Am series where she finished ninth in the point standings. She retired soon after. But she still thrills to see the successes of female drivers who have followed in the trails she blazed.

SHIRLEY MULDOWNEY: QUEEN OF DRAG RACERS

Shirley Muldowney—a petite brunette, 5'4", 110 pounds— has done more than compete in what had formerly been an exclusively male world. She has dominated that world. The sport is drag racing, and Shirley is one of the greatest of all time.

Shirley Roques was born on June 19, 1940, in Schenectady, New York, the daughter of a pro boxer. She remembers her dad letting her sit on his lap to "help him steer" as he drove fast down country roads.

Her high school sweetheart was Jack Muldowney, a local hot-rodder who taught Shirley how to drive when she was 16. The first time she ever got behind the wheel of Jack's Mercury, she made the speedometer needle push all the way to 120 mph. Some other boyfriend might have

Race car drivers tend to be macho, so it was a surprise when Shirley Muldowney showed up in a bright pink dragster. Regardless of how they looked, Shirley and her car's supercharged 2,000-horsepower engine made a habit of blowing away all the competition.

panicked had his girlfriend taken her first driving lesson at 120 mph, but not Jack. He could tell a natural when he saw one.

At 17, she quit high school and married Jack. A year later they had a son, John. At first, it looked like Shirley and Jack were the perfect couple. She wanted to drive hot rods and he wanted to be a mechanic at the dragstrip. Together, they would chase their dreams. Shirley's first car was a 1940 Ford Coupe that cost her $40. Her husband souped it up with a Cadillac engine, and off to the track they went. Jack was happy racing on weekends on the local track, but Shirley wanted to move on to the big-time. This difference eventually led to their divorce.

Taking son John with her on the road, Shirley purchased a Funny Car—a glamorous fiberglass dragster built to look like a factory model car—from well-known driver Conrad "Connie" Kalitta. That sale began a seven-year partnership between Shirley and Connie, during which he acted as her agent and helped turn her into a star. He billed her as Shirley "Cha Cha" Muldowney. She always hated that name.

Connie was the one who got Shirley onto the drag strips, but it was Shirley who won the races. By the end of her first full-time Funny Car season in 1971, she was ranked in the top five in the nation, and she had defeated just about all of the other top drivers at least once.

Shirley made it all the way to the finals of the National Hot Rod Association (NHRA) Nationals, the Super Bowl of drag racing, in 1971, and used her prize money to buy the Mustang Mach I she would race with the following season.

In the spring of 1972, Shirley's engine exploded in flames twice during races. Both times she escaped injury, but she showed guts and earned a lot of respect around the strip for it.

She had been lucky, but that luck ran out at the Nationals in Indianapolis in 1973. Her engine exploded again, and Shirley stayed with the car even as the fire spread into the cockpit. Medical attention rushed to the scene. Son John, now 14, ran to his mother's aid. She wasn't in good shape. When she climbed out of the car her helmet had been on fire. The fire had been so hot that her goggles had melted to her face, and she later had to have plastic surgery to remove the worst of the scars around her eyes. Those scars can barely be seen today, but Shirley, to this day, prefers to wear sunglasses when making a public appearance.

When Shirley recovered from her injuries and returned to racing in 1974, she moved onto Top Fuel dragsters, the long pointy-nosed dragsters that go faster over a quarter-mile than any other cars in the world. Five-thousand horsepower live in a Top Fuel engine. Just to give you an idea of how much that is, the typical stock car only generates about 700 horsepower.

Shirley describes what it's like to be behind the wheel of a Top Fuel dragster: "When you put that thing in gear boy, it kicks you like you can't believe! It just shoots!"

She became the first woman ever to break the six-second barrier for a quarter-mile in a dragster. At the end of the 1974 season she was voted a place on the American Auto Racing Writers and Broadcasting Association's Auto Racing All-

Shirley Muldowney (left) takes a break on the set of Heart Like a Wheel, *with actress Bonnie Bedelia. Bedelia played Muldowney in the movie.*

In 1984, Muldowney was severely injured in an accident and had to use a wheelchair to get around. Still, 19 months later, she announced she was returning to competition.

American Team. She again made history during the 1977 season when she became the first driver to win three national events in a row. That year, she won the 1977 NHRA Top Fuel World Championship.

At the end of the 1977 season, Shirley and Connie Kalitta went their separate ways. Now it was Shirley's turn to prove to all of her doubters that she could win without Connie Kalitta supervising her every move. Son John was now old enough to be one of mom's crew members. She scrimped and saved and they lived frugally, living from race to race. The 1978 and 1979 seasons were not noteworthy.

By 1980, however, Shirley was back in stride. That was the year she set the speed record for the quarter-mile with a 255-mph run in Pomona, California. She went on to win the NHRA Nationals in 1980, thus becoming the first driver to ever win that competition more than once.

A dramatic moment in Shirley's career came in 1982 at the Labor Day U.S. Nationals. She made it to the finals and her last opponent of the competition would be . . . Connie Kalitta! She ended up beating her former partner to the finish line by 9/100s of a second, 5.57 seconds to 5.66 seconds. It was the fastest side-by-side race ever run, and Shirley won it. After that, nothing could top her and she easily went on to win her third World Championship.

In 1983, Shirley's life was immortalized by Hollywood in the film *Heart Like a Wheel*, directed by Jonathan Kaplan, with Bonnie Bedelia playing Shirley and Beau Bridges playing Connie Kalitta.

In 1984, disaster struck. On June 29, Shirley was competing at a drag strip near Montreal, Canada, when her Top Fuel dragster blew a front tire. The car began to roll over and when it came to a stop it was nothing more than a twisted lump of scrap metal, with Shirley still inside. Her legs had multiple fractures. Five fingers, a hand, and her pelvis were broken. Her right thumb and left foot were nearly severed and had to be reattached during extensive surgery.

Shirley made a comeback in 1986. She could no longer bend her left foot, but a specially-built boot allowed her to drive. The comeback was short-lived, however, and Shirley retired for what seemed like good.

Ah, but the racing bug is not an easy one to get rid of. In 1996, Shirley returned to active drag racing, now driving Top Fuel dragsters in races sanctioned by the International Hot Rod Association (IHRA). Shirley is now struggling with a inadequate dragster that has a 1988 chassis—but delivery on her new dragster is expected any day now.

Never count this lady out.

SHELLY ANDERSON: RESPECT THE POWER

As is evidenced by the success of Shirley Muldowney, women have found a greater acceptance and success rate in drag racing than they have in any other form of motorsports. In addition to Shirley, three other women have won in a professional category at an NHRA national event: Shelly Anderson, Lucille Lee, and Lori Johns.

Shelly, now 30, is a current drag racing star, and has been ranked in the top 10 in the NHRA Winston points standings. Her biggest career win thus far came on May 5, 1996, in the Pennzoil Nationals in Richmond, Virginia. In the eliminations, she defeated points leader Rance McDaniel and five-time champion Joe Amato. Then in the finals, she smoked Scott Kalitta, the two-time defending top fuel champion, with a run of 4.779 seconds, or 298.90 mph.

Shelly comes from a racing family. Her father

Shelley Anderson is strapped in her dragster and ready for the green light.

Brad is a three-time NHRA Top Alcohol Funny Car champion, last winning in 1989. Brother Randy, who is a year older, won the Top Alcohol Funny Car titles in 1993 and 1994. Her oldest brother, Leigh, handled the engine-building business for Brad Anderson Enterprises from their home near Los Angeles, California. Mom, Carol, has many racing-related duties in addition to the "normal Mom stuff," including making race calculations and monitoring safety equipment.

Shelly and her brother Randy are both sponsored by Western Auto's Parts America.

Shelly went to college at Cal State-Fullerton, where she earned her degree in Communications in 1991. After school, she went racing.

"Racing was the only thing I wanted to do after college," she says today.

Even though she grew up around Funny Cars, she chose to compete in the Top Fuel Division.

"That's because Daddy says Funny Cars are for boys," Shelly says.

That piece of questionable wisdom aside, what is the best advice father Brad ever gave his daughter?

"Respect the power, or it'll hurt you," she says.

Shelly says that, even though she and her older brother are in the same sport, there really isn't any sibling rivalry. "There's no one I want to see win more than Randy," she says proudly.

A lot of people, when they have a bad day at work, can get away from it by going home. Of course, when you are in a family business, that isn't the case. "The family can get on your nerves," Shelly admits, but then quickly adds,

"But when you make a mistake, family is always there for you."

The Andersons' commitment to racing has left little time for other things. "We don't have a social life," Shelly says. "We are never home and the friends that Randy and I had in high school have given up on us."

Perhaps, but the world of racing is expecting big things of Shelly Anderson.

LYN ST. JAMES: SPIRIT OF THE AMERICAN WOMAN

Ever since she was a little girl, Lyn St. James has enjoyed being in motion.

"When I couldn't sleep as a child," she says, "my mother would take me for a ride in the car. I also used to rock my high chair across the kitchen. My mother would be doing the dishes and turn around to find me on the other side of the room."

Her obsession with moving—moving fast—continues to this day. She cannot talk about racing without revealing her passion.

"You wear the car," she says. "Every fiber of your body is with that car. Everything gets transmitted up through the tires, through the suspension and the seat, into your body. It's a very sensitive, precise experience. It's driving by the seat of your pants."

She was born Evelyn Cornwall, in Willoughby, Ohio, the lone child of the owners of a sheet

Lyn St. James dons her racing gear as she prepares for the ITT Automotive Detroit Grand Prix in 1993.

27

metal company. She has taken piano lessons since she was six, earned her piano-teaching certificate from the St. Louis Institute of Music, and is still today an accomplished classical pianist.

Lyn first learned of her love for racing when she was in her junior year of high school. She went to a drag strip to watch some of her friends race. Being a cocky kid, she laughed at them when they were eliminated.

They said, "If you're so smart, why don't you try?"

She did—and she won! Right then and there, that same night. But it wouldn't be until eight years later, in 1974, that she would become a professional auto racer. While in her early twenties, Lyn worked for a time as a secretary in Cleveland, Ohio, and taught piano on the side. She satisfied her thirst for speed by racing a coworker to work each morning in her Pontiac.

When she was 23 she married John Caruso, a racing fan. After her divorce, she took the name Lyn St. James, because she liked the actress Susan St. James who was then starring with Rock Hudson in the television series "MacMillan & Wife."

Lyn won the SCCA Florida Regional Showroom Stock A championship in 1976 and 1977. She then moved on to compete in the International Motor Sports Association (IMSA) Kelly American Challenge Series from 1979 to 1981, and she was named the top woman driver in that series for all three years.

In 1983 she raced in the SCCA Trans Am tour and finished tenth overall in the points race. The

St. James signs an autograph at the Indianapolis Motor Speedway.

following year she was named the Rookie of the Year in the IMSA Camel GT series by Autoweek magazine.

In September 1985, at the Watkins Glen road course in the Southern Tier of New York State, Lyn became the first woman to win a pro road race driving solo. The memory isn't entirely happy one for Lyn, however. Her crew—which should have been celebrating madly, popping the corks out of champagne bottles and giving Lyn lots of hugs and kisses—instead decided to be male chauvinist pigs and refused to join her in the winner's circle. Lyn still doesn't like to talk about it.

"I don't know why they didn't come," she says. "That's a real hard one. There could be a lot of reasons."

As Lyn's success grew, she found that she was no longer burdened by crews that were less than supportive. Chauvinists still sometimes tell her that she has no business being in a male sport, but, more and more, she finds that men give her the respect she is due, sometimes even confessing that there is no way that they could do what she does.

Two months after her Watkins Glen victory, on November 26, 1985, she set another record, becoming the first woman to break the 200-mph barrier on an oval track. She was timed at 204.233 mph in a Ford Mustang Probe prototype at the Talladega Superspeedway. That was also the season that Lyn became the first woman to win an IMSA GTO race, sharing the driving duties with John Johns in a race in Elkhart Lake, Wisconsin. She was named IMSA's "Most Improved Driver" for the 1985 season. She and Jones teamed for another GTO victory in the season finale in Daytona, a win sufficient to earn Lyn the Norelco Cup, naming her the GTO Driver of the Year.

In 1987, Lyn teamed with drivers Tom Gloy, Bill Elliott, and Scott Pruett to win the GTO division of the 24 Hours of Daytona endurance race.

The following year she broke her own women's speed record by turning a lap at 212.577 mph at Talladega in a Ford Thunderbird Super Coupe that had been put together for her by stock-car legend Bill Elliott's team.

In 1988, Lyn established 16 national and international speed records. In the SCCA Trans Am series that year, her consistency paid off. Lyn was the only driver to score championship points in every race. Her best finish that year was third in a race in Long Beach, California. That tied her with racer Deborah Gregg for best finish by a woman in a Trans Am event.

St. James talks with Hall of Fame golfer Carol Mann after St. James had just averaged over 221 miles per hour at the Texas World Speedway in 1992.

The highlight of Lyn's 1989 season was her first run in the 24 Hours of LeMans. She drove in the Trans Am series once again, and finished ninth in the points. Her best race was once again in Long Beach, a fourth place finish.

In 1990, Lyn teamed with drivers Robby Gordon, Calvin Fish, and Robert Lappalainen to win the GTO division of the 24 Hours of Daytona. The car finished fifth overall.

She also teamed with Gordon and Fish to win

the GTO division of the 12 Hours of Sebring race in a car that finished sixth overall. She finished a disappointing 14th in the Trans Am series that year, but she did have fourth place finishes in races at Phoenix, Portland, and Denver.

The most important thing that happened to Lyn in 1990, however, didn't have anything to do with a race. She met former Indianapolis 500 driver and current Indy-car owner Dick Simon. Simon knew talent when he saw it. He hired Lyn in November to test cars for Dick Simon Racing at the Brickyard. Once Lyn had a taste of the two-and-a-half mile quadrangle in Speedway, Indiana, she knew that she had to race in the Indianapolis 500, the greatest of all car races.

Lyn tried off-road racing in 1991, debuting in the Gold Coast 300 in Las Vegas, driving a Flare-side Ford F-150. Her ride was part of a special project sponsored by Ford Truck Operations. That was also the year that she made her debut in open-wheeled cars, driving a Formula 3 car in the U.S. Grand Prix in Phoenix, Arizona. She once again traveled to France to race in the 24 Hours of LeMans, this time as part of an all-woman team.

On the third day of time trials for the 1992 Indianapolis 500, Lyn—then 45 years old—accomplished a lifetime goal. She qualified for the starting grid in her Lola-Chevy at 11:16 AM on May 6, 1992, with a four-lap, 10-mile average speed of 220.150 mph. She would start the race on the outside of Row 9, in 27th position. She was the oldest rookie ever to qualify.

Earlier in the qualifying day, she had run a practice lap at 219.796 mph, thus reclaiming the women's closed course speed record, by exceeding the previous record of 217.498 mph set by Patty Moise in a Buick Regal in 1990 at Talladega.

Lyn was only the second woman to qualify for the race—Janet Guthrie being the first. Before her run, Lyn hadn't been at all nervous and spent her time in the garage area laughing and joking with reporters.

The following Sunday, the powers that be at the Indianapolis Motor speedway had a problem. Traditionally, the pre-race laps were commenced thunderously with the words, "Gentlemen, start your engines."

With a women in the starting field, what to do? When Janet Guthrie raced at Indy, the order to start engines had been the long-winded: "In the company of the first lady ever to qualify, gentlemen . . . "

Lyn had given the matter quite a bit of thought over the years, and understandably came up with the most sensible suggestion. "Just say, 'Drivers, start your engines.'" But when the time came for the famous words, Mrs. Mary Fendrich Hulman, widow of the long-time owner of the Speedway, Tony Hulman, read, instead, "Lady and Gentlemen, start your engines."

The race itself was not one that most fans will remember fondly. Many cars had tire problems due to the unusually cool day (56 degrees, 36 degrees with the windchill). Many drivers found it impossible to keep their cars off Indianapolis's unforgiving concrete walls, and the ambulance made numerous trips onto the track during the day. Several drivers were injured, the most seriously being Jeff Andretti who suffered severe injuries to his feet and ankles after his car hit the wall nose first.

By the end of the race, only 12 of the original 33 cars were still racing—but Lyn St. James was one of them.

She had negotiated the 2 1/2-mile quadrangle perfectly, finishing 193 laps by the finish. She finished eleventh, missing by two positions a chance to tie Janet Guthrie's record finish by a woman (ninth place, 1978).

"I just want to do it again!" were her first words after the race. "Ahhh! What a great feeling!"

Her car-owner, Dick Simon, had nothing but praise for his driver: "I thought Lyn did a magnificent job. She watched the temperatures in the car to keep the engine warm and she kept the tires hot by zigzagging. She didn't forget very much. She was competitive all day. She ran very strong and very consistent."

After qualifying for the 1992 Indy 500, St. James acknowledges the applause of her fellow drivers.

Her performance was good enough to win her the coveted Rookie of the Year Award. When it came time for her to go to the banquet and accept her award, she was a little bit concerned. Would men boo her?

Perhaps remembering the way she was snubbed by her own team following her first win at Watkins Glen, she was thrilled to find that: "My whole crew showed up! They showed at dinner and they came to my apartment afterward. As for my peers, when they announced I won the award, not only did the audience of 600 stand up, but the other 32 drivers gave me a standing ovation, rumored to be started by A. J. Foyt."

More than a year later, Lyn described how she felt inside that race car during her debut at The Brickyard: "I was in that perfect flow where I was hardly conscious of anything, just the car and the race."

The press has learned to love Lyn's truthfulness and willingness to talk about aspects of her sport from which the male drivers usually steer clear.

"Of course, the only thing that interrupted that concentration," Lyn continued, "was that I had to pee so bad. It was terrible. I drank a lot of water before the race, like I usually do, because your body is really working very hard in there and loses a lot of water. But it was a very cold day and I wasn't sweating as much as usual. Obviously, you can't take a bathroom break in the middle of the race, and I couldn't let it break my cocoon of concentration . . . "

So, what did she do?

"I peed," Lyn says with a grin. "Luckily, nothing short-circuited."

Lyn didn't do as well in her second Indy 500. She managed to run a 222 mph lap on the second day of time trials for the fastest speed of the day, and qualified her number 90 1993 Lola-Ford Cosworth, which she had named "Spirit of the American Woman"—on the outside of the seventh row (21st position) with a speed of 218.042 mph.

Race day, however, left her disappointed. Her transmission conked out with 21 laps remaining. Her car limped to a stop at the entrance to Pit Road, causing a yellow caution flag to come out. She finished 25th.

"This sport really beats you up and breaks your heart," she said after the race. "You work all year at getting everything right. Then something like a 25-cent O-ring blows and you're done."

Lyn executed her best qualifying run ever at Indy in 1994, driving her Lola-Ford around the Brickyard four times at an average speed of 224.154 mph. (That means she covered the 10-mile distance in about 2 minutes and 41 seconds.) The time was good enough for her to start the race on the outside of the second row in sixth position.

In the race, Lyn accomplished her goal of finishing the race, but well off the winning pace. She finished in 19th place.

Lyn's 1995 Indy 500 was a short one. On the first lap, Stan Fox was involved in a horrifying crash when his car slammed into the wall head first in turn one and then was sheared in half by Eddie Cheever's car. Debris from the crash, which left Fox near death with a severely fractured skull, hit Lyn's car and put her out of commission. She was out of the race before she had a chance to run through the second turn.

Officially, she finished the race last, apparently because her car stopped on the track behind the wrecks of Cheever and Fox.

Lyn started 1996 intending to run a full schedule with the new Indy Racing League (IRL), which had formed as direct competition to the IndyCar Racing Series. One of the benefits of joining the new league was that, come Memorial Day, IRL drivers were guaranteed 25 starting positions in the field for the Indianapolis 500.

Her year got off to a good start when she finished eighth in the first-ever Indy 200 at Walt

Disney World in Florida. Her luck turned, however, when she crashed in practice when Buddy Lazier spun out in front of her at Phoenix, forcing her to use her backup car for that race. The crash slightly injured Lyn, but it put Buddy Lazier in the hospital for weeks with 17 fractures in his backbone.

Lyn started 22nd in Phoenix and finished 21st. She only completed 10 laps when her car broke down because of electrical problems.

She had a parting of the ways with the team she had started the season with and showed up at Indianapolis with a brand new team and a brand new sponsor. She would be driving a pink and black #45 1994 Lola for Zunne Group Racing and McCormack Motorsports, and one of her sponsors would be Lifetime, the cable network for women. The car is called "The Spirit of San Antonio."

Although the last-minute change might have put her behind some of the other teams at Indy, she was in far better shape than she had been in previous years, when she would show up at the Brickyard still begging for sponsorship.

"It's nice to come here and not have to worry about finding sponsors," Lyn said on the final day of practice in 1996. "Now I can concentrate on driving the car and doing the job that needs to be done."

Lyn's car may be the first at Indy with pink as part of its color scheme. "I'm a lady driver and the Family Channel is a lady's channel, so we thought pink would be appropriate," Lyn said as she signed autographs along Pit Road.

Lyn's best lap during practice was only in the neighborhood of 215 mph, 24 mph off the best times being turned in by the hot cars, the

Menards, driven by Arie Luyendyck, Scott Bray-ton, and rookie phenom Tony Stewart. St. James's team still had a lot of work to do.

Along with Lyn's newcomer status with her car and team, another factor in that speed gap was the weather. Forty-nine hours of practice were scheduled before the qualification attempts began, but less than half of those were actual-ly held because of rain.

When the first day of qualifying arrived, on May 11, 1996, it was announced that the min-imum qualification speed to make the field would be 220 mph. That meant that Lyn was going to have to increase her best lap of the month by five mph in order to make the field. When the lottery was drawn to determine the qualification order, Lyn drew number one. She would be the first one onto the track once qualification began.

But when would that be? A morning shower delayed the scheduled noon start for qualifying. Then, just before qualification was to begin, a 30-minute practice session was scheduled, so drivers could get used to the track conditions they were going to have to qualify under.

The 30-minute practice session meant 30 min-utes of green-flag practicing; the clock stopped every time a yellow flag came out to slow the cars down. The cars had only been practicing for two minutes when the first yellow came out.

This was due to Johnny Parsons, Jr., hitting the wall. He spun out coming out of Turn Three and stuck the outer wall with his right rear. This knocked off his right-rear tire. The tire went bouncing across the track and clipped Arie Luyendyk's car as he tried to get past. Parsons was okay but his car was demolished. Luyendyk's car was not damaged in the accident, but later had engine problems, thus ending Arie's dreams of sitting on the pole for the race.

Two of the cars owned by A. J. Foyt blew engines in separate incidents after the green flag came back out, and this further delayed things. It was 3:00 PM by the time Lyn finally took the track for her qualification attempt.

Then she nailed it.

Her average speed for her four times around the Brickyard was 224.594 mph, good enough to put her in 18th position, on the outside of the sixth row, for the big race.

The mood around Indy turned somber on May 17, 1996 when Scott Brayton, while testing a backup car, crashed in Turn Two and was killed.

On raceday, less than a half hour before Lyn was to climb into her car for the race, she was asked if this Indy was going to be different for her.

"Other than the fact that I have a woman co-car owner [Barbie Siever] and a sponsorship that is fully supporting me, things aren't a whole lot different this year," Lyn said. "I have always had a lot of women supporting me, and I've always been appreciative of that."

Soon the time for chatting with reporters was over. "Today, I have a race to win, and that's what I'll be concentrating on," she concluded.

The race got off to a clean start, but Lyn's car was immediately off the lead pace. Drivers who were behind Lyn radioed in to their pit crews that her car was "puffing oil." The car hung in there and didn't break down, but it was clear from the start that there was going to be no run to the front for Lyn St. James on this day. She dropped back to 26th place, but at the halfway mark, so many other drivers had been forced to leave, she moved into the 16th position.

Then, just after Lyn completed her 153rd lap (of a scheduled 300) her car came together with the #44 Reynard-Ford driven by Scott Harrington. The two cars both hit the wall and slid to a stop side by side but facing in opposite directions.

Lyn suffered a broken right wrist, but she was able to walk to the ambulance. Harrington was uninjured. Officially, Lyn's 153 completed laps earned her 14th place in the race. As far as her ultimate dream goes, the dream of winning the Indianapolis 500, her motto must remain: "Wait till next year."

What will she do to fill her time until the next race? Well . . .

A wife and mother, Lyn has always been active outside of her duties behind the wheel of a race car. She is or has been a consumer advisor for the Ford Motor Company, a commentator for the ESPN and Showtime cable networks (work for which she was nominated for an ACE Award in 1989), president of the Woman's Sports Foundation, the author of a book, *Lyn St. James' Car Owners' Manual*, a columnist for the *Detroit Free Press, Cosmopolitan*, and *Seventeen* magazines, and a corporate spokesperson for the Ford Motor Company and Rolex. She was three times invited to the White House as the guest of Presidents Ronald Reagan and George Bush, and she is the owner of her own sales and marketing firm, LSJ Motorsports. Even off the track, she moves fast.

PATTY MOISE: CHIP OFF THE OLD BLOCK

Patty Moise was born on December 29, 1960, in Jacksonville, Florida, the daughter of road-racer driver Milton Moise. The 5'7", 120-pound brunette graduated from Jacksonville University. She began her professional racing career as a road racer, just like her dad. She drove sedans in the IMSA American Challenge Series. She won her first race in 1986 in Portland, Oregon.

She made her National Association of Stock Car Automobile Racing (NASCAR) Busch Grand National (BGN) debut in 1986 at Road Atlanta and qualified for the third spot on the starting grid. Unfortunately, her engine blew before she could complete the first lap.

She was luckier at Road Atlanta the following year. On this track a qualifying record was a speed faster than 176 mph. She finished in

Patty Moise has set numerous racing records. She is also the first woman to be an owner/driver for a NASCAR racing team.

eighth place for that race, her best finish up until that time.

Also in 1987, Patty won the Winn-Dixie Challenge Qualifying Race at Charlotte Motor Speedway and made her debut on the Winston Cup circuit, the major leagues of stock car racing, finishing tenth at Martinsville and eleventh at Rockingham. She was the first woman to ever race on the Martinsville track, the oldest track used by NASCAR.

Patty ran in three more Winston Cup races in 1988—the Winston Open, Firecracker 400 at Daytona, and the Budweiser at the Glen road race at Watkins Glen—and she finished all three.

That same year, she also won the pole position for both of the American Race Car Association (ARCA) races run at the Talladega Superspeedway. The late Davey Allison is the only other person to accomplish that feat. Patty, in the process, became the first woman in oval-track history to win a pole position on a superspeedway.

She raced in three more Winston Cup races in 1989 and also won the pole position in the ARCA 200 at Daytona.

Perhaps Patty's greatest moment came on January 23, 1990, when she set the world oval-track speed record for a woman. She was timed around the two-and-a-half tri-oval at Talladega at an average speed of 217.498 mph. In November of that year, Patty married stock car driver Elton Sawyer.

Patty ran only a limited schedule on the Busch Grand National circuit until 1990, when she went full time, racing in 24 Busch races that year.

She lost her sponsorship after the 1990 season and raced only six times total in 1991 and 1992. The highlight of her 1992 season was a lap of 217.498 mph at the Talladega Superspeedway in Talladega, Alabama, thus setting the women's closed-course speed record. (Her record held until practicing commenced for that year's Indianapolis 500, when Lyn St. James broke the record with a lap of 219.796 mph at the Brickyard.)

Patty sat out the 1993 season and then returned a year later, once again on a limited schedule, now with a sponsorship from Dial-Purex. In 1994, Patty again ran the Busch series full time and qualified for 24 races.

In 1995, Patty drove for Doug Taylor Motorsports. It was during this season that she accomplished her best finish in a race, seventh-place at Talladega—the site of her speed record. That finish earned her the biggest single-race paycheck she has ever achieved, $11,175.

Moise left the team at the end of the 1995 season to form her own team, and she took crew chief Mike Hillman with her. She attended all 26 Busch Grand National races in 1995 and qualified for 22 of them. She finished 25th in the

Moise oversees the preparation of her tires as she prepares to run in the 1989 Arca 200 at Daytona Beach. Moise was the first woman ever to win the pole position at Daytona.

BGN point standings and earned $98,086.

In 1996 she drove for the first time in a car—the Dial-Purex Ford—which she co-owned with her husband. She has became the first woman to be both the driver and owner of her race car.

In the meantime, husband Elton Sawyer has moved up to the Winston Cup circuit, driving the David Blair Motorsports Ford Thunderbird. (Sawyer was released by Blair halfway through the season as the racing firm needed to cut back to a part-time schedule and wanted to give Sawyer the opportunity to find another full-time ride.)

Can two race car drivers be married to one another and not drive each other crazy?

"Absolutely," Patty says. "Because this sport is so time consuming, I think it would be hard for anyone who wasn't a racer to understand the commitment. I don't think any other husband would understand. We share experiences and talk about the things we learn. When things get to be too much, we can put it aside . . . like the famous line from *Gone With the Wind,* 'We'll deal with that tomorrow.'"

Of course, a couple as busy as this can fall behind on the chores at home every now and again. "We didn't get around to mowing the lawn for a long time," Patty says. "Then Elton tried to do it at 9:30 at night, the only time we had available. The neighbors weren't thrilled."

As for being new car owners, Patty likens it to being new parents. "This is our baby," she says, referring to the Dial-Purex T-Bird that Patty drives.

They see the car as their security. When they retire as active drivers they hope to own cars and put young racers in them. "We want to find the new Elton and Patty," they say.

Along with racing, Patty enjoys riding and competing with horses. She is now a TV broadcaster as well, having joined the SuperStation WTBS Motorsports announcing crew for Winston Cup races.

6

SHAWNA ROBINSON: "SOME THINK IT'S A MANLY THING"

Born and raised in Des Moines, Iowa, Shawna Robinson is the daughter of Richard Robinson, an amateur weekend racer who enjoyed tinkering on a car (or five) on the front lawn.

He encouraged all of his children to become racers. As youngsters, he taught them to race on minibikes, motorcycles, and snowmobiles.

"I still have the burn marks on my legs from motorcycle racing as a teenager," Shawna says with a hint of pride. Battle scars.

Her first racing series was driving in the truck division at a local short track. Five years later she began to race in NASCAR-sanctioned events.

Even though Shawna Robinson is a pretty blonde who wouldn't look out of place walking down the beach, inside the glamorous exterior is the fierce determination of a warrior. Because

Shawna Robinson prepares for the start of the 1994 Busch Light 300. She led all qualifiers and started from the pole position.

of that determination, Shawna became the first woman to win a NASCAR touring event when she took the checkered flag at the new Asheville Speedway in 1988. That same year she became the first woman to win the Most Popular Driver award in the Charlotte/Daytona Dash Series. She was 23.

Shawna's first start in a Busch Grand National (BGN) race came on June 8, 1991, in Rougemont, North Carolina. She started from the pole position once in her BGN career, on March 10, 1994, at age 29, in the Busch Light 300 at the Atlanta Motor Speedway. It was a race she will never forget.

The good part of the race was that she won the pole position with her qualifying run in her orange Polaroid Chevrolet. In fact, she also set a new BGN track record with a speed of 174.330 mph. Simply for winning the pole, she earned a purse of $5,037, her biggest earnings to date.

Sitting next to her on the front row was gentleman Joe Nemechek, the 1992 BGN champion, who gave Shawna a red rose in Atlanta's Victory Lane during the pole-position ceremonies.

Nemechek clearly thought of Shawna as a worthy opponent—but not all the other drivers on the track did. Some men can turn vicious when they feel threatened by a woman.

On the very first lap, Shawna and Nemechek were entering Turn Three side by side when Mike Wallace moved alongside Shawna's car on the inside so that the three cars were going through the turn three abreast. This move by Wallace took the air off Shawna's spoiler, a wing at the back of the car that collects air as it moves over the car and uses it to keep the car on the track. This made her car aerodynamically unstable.

Before putting on on her safety helmet, Robinson checks her earpiece so she can hear instructions from her crew.

She was sandwiched by two cars into a vacuum that threw her car out of balance. She drifted up the track and into Nemechek. Together, the two front row cars went into the retaining wall. Nemechek's car was totaled, out of the race. Shawna had severe front end damage but her crew sawed a lot of the sheet metal away and she limped around the track in the slow lane for 63 laps, her engine showing. Then her radiator broke and she, too, called it quits.

Nemechek was furious with Wallace and did something that seemed to come straight out of pro wrestling. He went to the public address announcer and grabbed his microphone. In an angry voice, he addressed the large and stunned crowd. He told them that Wallace was a gutless so-and-so who had purposefully made Shawna crash.

"I'd heard from people before the race that he was going to take some air off her spoiler and get her loose," Nemechek told a reporter after the race. "I figured he was just running his mouth, but he did just that. Going three-across on the first lap is a big risk. People could have gotten hurt. You don't pull a stunt like that."

Just about that same time Shawna and Wallace's wife Karla had to be separated, as they got into an ugly shouting match. A reporter asked Shawna why Wallace did it.

"Ego," she said. "Maybe some think it's a manly thing. I don't know where that thinking comes from. How many fans were taking bets? Is the girl going to crash on the first lap? By starting on the pole and racing well I had hoped I could have changed those attitudes. I've never wanted to flaunt the woman thing. I just want to be thought of as a good driver, not a good female driver."

Wallace denied purposefully making Shawna crash. One photographer, who was on the scene at the time of the accident, delivered his opinion concisely: "He took her out." However, NASCAR officials reviewed the incident and determined that there was "no blame."

Shawna pressed on with her season. Her best finish in a BGN race was a tenth-place finish in Watkins Glen, New York, on June 25, 1994. To date, her BGN career earnings are $138,951.

Robinson's last BGN race came at Road Atlanta in Atlanta, Georgia on March 11, 1995. Was it the good-old-boy network that drove her out of racing? No. Shawna and her husband were expecting a baby.

Even though it was discovered, to everyone's horror, that there is no rule on the NASCAR books saying that a pregnant person can't drive a stock car, Shawna has voluntarily put her career on hiatus. Since then, she has had a baby boy. She is also working as an interior decorator these days, her clients being many of the drivers and car owners in the Charlotte, North Carolina area.

In addition to Patty Moise and Shawna Robinson, three other women have raced in BGN competition. The first woman to do it was Diane Teel, who broke the gender barrier on March 28, 1982, in Martinsville, Virginia. Diane was born on February 16, 1948, in Seaford, Virginia, so she got to make her BGN debut in her home state. She made ten BGN starts in all, her last being almost exactly two years after her first, and at the same track. She ran her last BGN race on March 25, 1984, at Martinsville. Her best finish was an eighth-place in Hampton, Virginia. Her best qualification run earned her a 12th-place starting position for that same race. Diane's biggest single-race purse was $1,000 at Martinsville on March 20, 1983.

Debby Lunsford—born June 23, 1963, in Gainesville, Georgia—started one BGN race on May 13, 1989, in her home town. She started 15th and finished 23rd, winning $550 in prize money.

Lisa Jackson—born October 12, 1961, in Arden, North Carolina—started one race in Asheville, North Carolina, on June 11, 1982. She both started and finished 17th and won $220 for her efforts.

Only six times have two women drivers been in a BGN race at the same time—twice each in 1991, 1994, and 1995. All six times, the women involved were Patty Moise and Shawna Robinson.

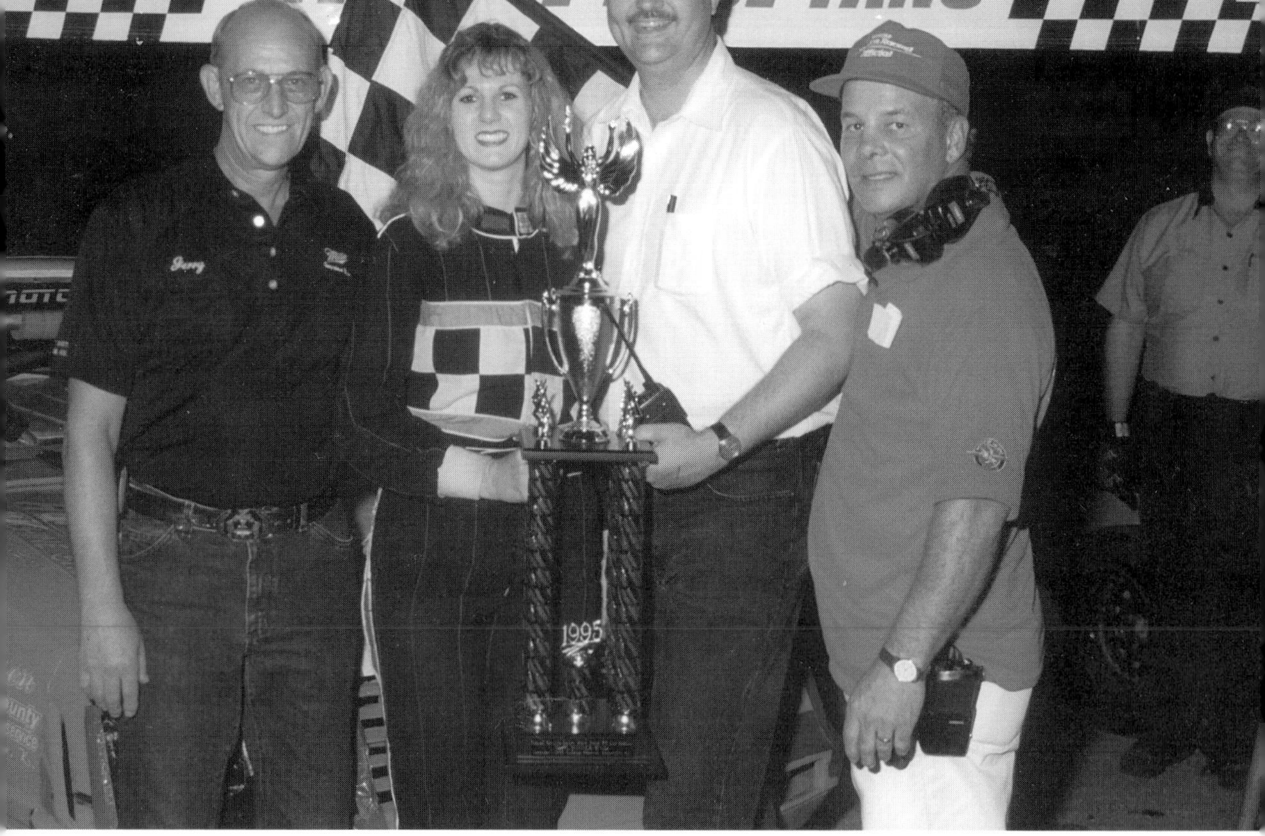
Genuine Draf
FANS
1995

7

WOMEN OF SATURDAY NIGHT

O f course, not all female race car drivers have become household names. The great majority of them, like their male counterparts, take their race car to the local quarter-mile track on weekends with dreams of one day racing at Indianapolis or Talladega or Daytona. Here are a few notable up-and-comers.

JENNIFER COBB

Jennifer Cobb, 23, first got interested in racing when her dad, Joey Cobb, started driving stock cars when she was three years old.

"I was a real racetrack rugrat," says Jennifer. "I pretty much grew up at the racetrack. Then

Along with her victory trophy, Jennifer Cobb celebrates in Victory Lane with (from left to right) Jerry Hamilton, a representative from the race's sponsor; Bob Baker, the General Manager of Lakeside/I-70 Speedway; and Terry Wantland, flagman at Lakeside/I-70.

in high school I drifted away from it for a while. I was a cheerleader for the football team, and I was dating and stuff like that. Then a friend of mine fixed me up with a car for the Pony Stock class when I was 18. I was afraid to ask my dad because I thought he wouldn't let me drive it, but he just said, 'Let's check it out.' So, we checked out the car. I only raced in four races that season [1991] and then I crashed and hurt my neck. It turned out the car was unsafe and that was when my dad decided to oversee my career. Since then, he has taught me to race to win every time. He has really instilled the winning attitude in my head. He's very tough on me but I wouldn't have it any other way."

She races at I-70 Speedway (located in Lenexa, Kansas) and Lakeside Speedway (Kansas City, Kansas).

So far in her career she has had three feature wins. Jennifer comments, "There should have been more. I've had guys put me out on the last lap. It's hard to say if they did it because I was a woman or not, but when a total stranger takes you out and they are in a slower car, then something must be up.

"Most of my competitors respect me and the female thing is not an issue," she continues. "But every once in a while you run into some immature driver. Guys who think like that are inevitably losers, because they are concentrating so hard on seeing to it that the girl doesn't win, that they lose any chance to win themselves. These are the same guys who spend more time looking at their rear-view mirror than they do at their windshield. At Lakeside and I-70 there are very few of these guys."

During the 1995 season, Jennifer finished fifth in the points at Lakeside Speedway in the Pony Stock division. For the 1996 season, she moved up to the Charger class, which is very similar to the Late Models. Her current race car is a 1996 Thunderbird with a Clevor engine.

"We've done okay this year, a lot better than we expected right out of the box," Jennifer said during the 1996 season. "We have three top-three finishes so far in feature races, and a couple of heat [preliminary] race wins, early in the season, but since then things have gone sour for us. A couple of blown motors and a couple of crashes have really made things tough. But I know that a feature win is coming soon. Our team is very capable."

Outside of racing, Jennifer is an account executive at Kross Office Outfitters in Overland Park, Kansas. She is also a student at the University of Kansas, where she is working toward her Bachelors degree. She enjoys dancing and working out.

"It's hard to get to the gym during the season," she says. "And that's when I need it the most."

In 1993, Jennifer was an alternate cheerleader for the Kansas City Chiefs football team. "I would like to try cheerleading again someday," she says, "but racing is definitely number one with me, and that doesn't leave much time for other things. I want to go as far as I can in racing. I won't give up on my dream, and I won't fail as long as I don't give up."

JENNIFER FRY

Eighteen-year-old Jennifer Fry of Honaker, Virginia, elects to give up her summer Saturday nights of dating or just "hanging out" to go racing in the Pure Stock division at the NASCAR Winston Racing Series-sanctioned Lonesome Pine International Raceway in Coeburn, Virginia. The 1996 campaign is her second full season of competition, and, as of June, she was in ninth place in the points standings for her division, driving a red, white, and blue 1982 Ford Fairmont. Out of the nearly 100 drivers who compete weekly at Lonesome Pine, Jennifer is the only woman.

Jennifer comes by her love of racing honestly. She was only four years old when her father, Greg, and two cousins started power-boat racing in

Eighteen-year-old Jennifer Fry of Honaker, Virginia, and her home-built Pure Stock Car.

Florida, where the family team won a state and world championship in 1992. The Fry family moved to southwestern Virginia in 1994, deep in the heart of the coal fields. Soon thereafter, a friend's father let Jennifer drive his car in a Ladies Enduro race, which features strictly stock cars with a roll cage added. In this type of race, there are no caution flags and the race continues around disabled or wrecked cars that have been left on the track.

In her first race, Jennifer, then 16, took third place. She was hooked. She and her father formed their own team called the J&D (Jennifer and Dad) Race Team and immediately went to work on building a pure stock car.

At first, her reception at the track wasn't all she had hoped it would be. "Some of the guys at the track weren't so helpful," she says politely. "I guess it was because I was so young and a girl on top of that."

A year of experience has made a big difference. Not only is she a much better driver today, but she has earned the respect of the drivers she competes against each week. "Our goal for 1996 is to finish in the top five in the points standings," she says. Helping this effort is the fact that she has obtained four sponsors for her car who help the team financially.

Jennifer is still in search of her first victory but hopes to take care of that soon. Her dream is to race on the NASCAR Winston Cup circuit. "My dad is an inspiration to me," she says. "He wants me to win a race almost as badly as I want to win one. He works hard on the race car almost every night, getting it ready for Saturday night's race. I work with him and he has taught me a lot about a race car. I can't say enough about him and how important he is to me.

"Although I haven't won a race yet, I have found a victory in myself because I have been able to come this far in a short period of time— and that means a lot to me."

The tradition of sending a beauty queen (left) to Victory Lane to kiss the winner (Angie Wilson, center) will need to be changed as women keep taking the checkered flag.

ANGIE WILSON

Angie Wilson of Marion, North Carolina, is only 21 years old but she is already a racing veteran. She began her speed career racing go-karts at the age of 14. In her second year as a racer, in 1990, she won more than 40 times at numerous tracks across the southeastern states, earning her the Pine Valley Speedway Junior Class Championship and the Junior Carolina Cup Sprint Series Championship.

In 1991, she moved to mini stock cars and won more than 20 races at various tracks. At the end of the 1991 season, she was awarded the Junior Driver of the Year Award at the Rockingham Motor Speedway. In 1992, in the Mini

Stock Division, she had five wins at the Hickory Motor Speedway and the Tri-County Motor Speedway, earning her the 1992 Rookie of the Year in the Mini Sport Division. She also won the 1992 Most Popular Driver award at Hickory and she became the first female to win a NASCAR-sanctioned race at Hickory.

The following year, 1993, was a transition year for Angie, as she moved from the Mini Sport Division to the Limited Division. In five races, she finished in the top five only once. As a rookie in the Limited Sportsman division in 1994, she won one heat race and had seven top-five finishes, good enough for a ninth-place finish in the points standings. In 1995, Angie became the first woman to win the Limited Sportsman Division at Tri-County Motor Speedway. In 1996, she moved up to the Late Model Division, once again competing as a rookie.

Angie is a senior at Western Carolina University and says that Mark Martin is her favorite racer.

"I see nothing different from a female and a male driver," says Angie, who currently races in both a Ford Thunderbird and a Chevrolet Monte Carlo. "Gender has nothing to do with who can make a car handle with speed." Anyone who has seen Angie race has to agree.

STATISTICS

JANET GUTHRIE'S INDY 500 RECORD

Year	Qual. speed	Start	Finish	Laps	Reason Out
1977	188.403	26	29	27	Broken gear
1978	190.325	15	9	190	Running

LYN ST. JAMES INDY 500 RECORD

Year	Qual. speed	Start	Finish	Laps	Reason Out
1992	220.150	27	11	193	Running
1993	218.042	21	25	176	Gear Box
1994	224.154	6	19	170	Running
1995	225.346	28	32	0	Accident

PATTY MOISE BUSCH GRAND NATIONAL RECORD

YEAR	STARTS	WINS	TOP 10	MONEY
1986	2	0	0	$ 1,210
1987	13	0	2	$12,718
1988	11	0	0	$10,861
1989	12	0	0	$12,615
1990	24	0	0	$40,683
1991	5	0	0	$ 6,295
1992	1	0	0	$ 1,825
1994	6	0	0	$18,920
1995	22	0	1	$96,086
CAREER	96	0	3	$201,213

CHRONOLOGY

1899   Mme. Labrouse of Paris, France drives in the Tour de France.

1901   Cammille du Gast races with 170 male drivers from Paris to Berlin, finishes 33rd.

1975   Lella Lombardi races an entire season on the Formula One (Grand Prix) circuit.

1977   Guthrie becomes first woman to race in the Indianapolis 500. Shirley Muldowney becomes first woman to win the NHRA Top Fuel World Championship.

1985   Lyn St. James becomes the first woman to win a pro road race driving solo; also becomes first woman to turn a lap at 200 mph on an oval track.

1988   Shawna Robinson becomes first woman to win a NASCAR touring event.

1992   St. James becomes oldest rookie to qualify for the Indianapolis 500.

1996   Patty Moise becomes first woman to both own and drive her race car.

SUGGESTIONS FOR FURTHER READING

Altmark, Barry C., "It's a Family Business: Patty Moise and Elton Sawyer," *Stock Car Spectacular*, September 1995.

Anderson, Dave, "Bath for Lady During Pit Stop," *The New York Times*, May 30, 1977.

Arneson, Sandy, "Andersons share passion for fast cars, family," *USA Today*, May 24, 1996.

Duden, Jane, *Shirley Muldowney*, Mankato: Minnesota: Crestwood House, 1988.

Lieber, Jill, "A Road Less Taken," *Sports Illustrated*, May 3, 1993.

Lieber, Jill, "Sports People: Shawna Robinson," *Sports Illustrated*, March 21, 1994.

Sarris, Eve, "A Woman on the Fast Track," *Newsday*, May 30, 1993.

ABOUT THE AUTHOR

Michael Benson is the editor of *Stock Car Spectacular* and *Stock Car Superstars* magazines. His previous books include *Vintage Science Fiction Films, Ballparks of North America, Dream Teams, Who's Who in the JFK Assassination, Monster Trucks, Pickup Trucks,* and *Muscle Cars.* He has also written *Crashes and Collisions* and *Dale Earnhardt* for Chelsea House's Race Car Legends Series. He is also the editor of the *Military Technical Journal.* A graduate of Hofstra University, Benson lives in Brooklyn, New York, with his wife, daughter, and son.

INDEX

PHOTO CREDITS
AP/Wide World Photos: 2, 8, 13, 16, 20, 26, 30; Courtesy NHRA: 6, 22; UPI/Bettmann: 11; Archive Photos: 19, 28, 33; Corbis, 43; copyright Barry Altmark: 46, 49; courtesy Angie Wilson: 58.